BAMBINO

and Mr. Twain

P. I. Maltbie

Illustrated by Daniel Miyares

🌉 Charlesbridge

To Dr. Arthur M. Axelrad, for preparing me to be an author.
And to Randi Rivers for making it happen.—P. I. M.

To Eva Esrum, for encouraging me to make pictures.—D. M.

Text copyright © 2012 by P. I. Maltbie
Illustrations copyright © 2012 by Daniel Miyares
All rights reserved, including the right of reproduction in whole or in part in any form.
Charlesbridge and colophon are registered trademarks of Charlesbridge Publishing, Inc.

Published by Charlesbridge
85 Main Street
Watertown, MA 02472
(617) 926-0329
www.charlesbridge.com

Library of Congress Cataloging-in-Publication Data
Maltbie, P. I.
   Bambino and Mr. Twain / P.I. Maltbie; illustrated by Daniel Miyares.
      p. cm.
   Summary: In 1904 Sam Clemens leads a reclusive life in New York City after the death of his wife, who
was also his editor, until his cat, Bambino, influences him to rejoin society. Includes brief notes on the life
and work of Samuel Langhorne Clemens, who was known to the world by his pen name, Mark Twain.
   ISBN 978-1-58089-272-8 (reinforced for library use)
1. Twain, Mark, 1835–1910—Juvenile fiction. [1. Twain, Mark, 1835–1910—Fiction. 2. Authors, American—
Fiction. 3. Cats—Fiction. 4. New York (N.Y.)—History—1898–1951—Fiction.] I. Miyares, Daniel, ill. II. Title.
PZ7.M29835Bam 2012
[E]—dc22   2011000653

Printed in Singapore
(hc) 10 9 8 7 6 5 4 3 2 1

Illustrations done in mixed media and digital
Display type set in Knock Out and text type set in Monotype Baskerville
Color separations by KHL Chroma Graphics, Singapore
Printed and bound September 2011 by Imago in Singapore
Production supervision by Brian G. Walker
Designed by Susan Mallory Sherman

On a gloomy November day in 1904,
a crowd gathered in front of a big house in New York City.

"Did you know Mark Twain lives here?"

"He's my favorite author!"

A woman with a broom appeared at the door, scowling at the people gathered outside.

A reporter pushed through the crowd. "I'm here from the *Herald* to interview Mr. Twain," he said.

"Mr. Clemens . . . I mean, Mr. Twain, can't be disturbed," the woman snapped. With that she slammed the door.

From an upstairs window an old man with wild white hair and a black cat watched the crowd walk away.

"Everyone wants to meet witty Mark Twain," the man said. "But tell me, Bambino, would they want to meet sad, old Samuel Clemens?"

Bambino hissed at the people walking away.

Katy Leary, Mr. Twain's housekeeper, entered the room. She scowled at Bambino before saying, "Mr. Clemens, I got rid of the crowd."

Samuel Clemens nodded. "You did the right thing, Katy."

After Katy left, Jean Clemens entered. "Papa," she said, "why don't you come downstairs? I just made some ice cream."

Jean smiled, but Sam could see her face was worn from grieving over her mother's death. She was growing old before her time. And his other daughter, Clara, was far away in a clinic—too upset by her mother's death to be with them.

"Well . . ."

"Just have a little," Jean coaxed. "Bambino can have some, too."

Sam picked up Bambino and followed Jean downstairs.

"Happy birthday, Mr. C.! I knew Miss Jean could get you out of your room," Katy said, smiling.

On the table were presents, stacks of mail, and a birthday cake with a lone candle.

"I thought we'd continue Mama's tradition of lighting a single candle," Jean said.

As Jean cut the cake, Sam remembered an earlier birthday, when his wife, Livy, was alive. . . .

"The girls and I decided you should have a single candle on your cake so you'll never grow old," Livy had said.

"Quite right, Livy," Sam had replied. "If you lit all the candles my age requires, we'd burn the house down."

Dear Livy, Sam thought. *She left us too soon. . . .*

"Papa," said Jean, pulling her father back to the present. "A few of your friends have invited you to dinner." Jean handed him an invitation from the pile of mail. "You should go."

"No," Sam said. "They'll only expect me to be funny. And I'm not anymore."

"Mother wouldn't want you to shut yourself up in the house," Jean said.

"Tell them I'm just too old and tired," Sam said.

"But Papa . . ."

Sam hit the table with his fist. "I don't want to see anyone!"

Jean and Katy exchanged a look.

"As you say, Mr. C.," Katy said, dishing out the ice cream.

Sam cleared his throat. "Since Clara can't be with us, we'll have her Bambino stand in for her," he said, giving a saucer of ice cream to the cat.

Bambino rubbed his head against Sam's hand, blinked his eyes, and then lapped up his treat.

As the days became colder and darker, Sam spent more time in bed, reading, writing, and grumbling. Bambino was always with him, although the bed was so littered with books and papers that the cat had difficulty finding a soft place to sleep.

"Mr. C., I don't know how you find anything on that bed," Katy scolded as she straightened up the mess.

"You could lose a cat on this bed," Sam agreed.

Katy reached for some papers, but Bambino hissed. "I know one cat I'd like to see lost," she muttered. "Permanently!"

Before long, snow started to fall. Jean and Katy decorated the rooms with greenery and red ribbons. Sam was invited to many parties, but he stayed home.

Often he wandered from room to room, looking for something to do. Sometimes he would gaze at a small picture of Livy.

Other times, Sam would play billiards—with Bambino.
When Sam shot the ball toward the cat, Bambino swatted it back.
   "Bambino, you'd make a champion billiards player if you
could only hold a cue," Sam said.

Snow turned to rain and spring arrived. Squirrels filled the trees, tormenting Bambino with their chatter. Katy bustled about opening windows to air out rooms.

One afternoon Bambino led Sam to an unused room. Jumping from boxes to trunks, he tried to catch a glittering sunbeam.

"Over there, Bambino! Wait . . . it's moved. . . ."

Bambino attacked the sunbeam dancing on the wardrobe door. Sam opened the door. The sunbeam shone on a white suit. Bambino swatted at it.

"I used to wear this every summer when Livy was alive," Sam said. "She said that it made me look young. Those were happy days."

Just then Bambino heard a squirrel chattering outside the open window. In an instant he was on the windowsill, and another jump landed him in the tree branches.

"Bambino, no!" Sam shouted, running to the window.

But Bambino didn't hear him. Seeing the squirrel that had been teasing him for days, Bambino chased it down to the street and around the corner.

"Bamb-i-i-i-n-o-o-o!"

Sam's voice echoed over the city noises.

LOST

MARK TWAIN'S CAT

BLACK CAT WITH THICK,
VELVETY FUR AND BLUE EYES,
NAMED **BAMBINO**.
A $5.00 REWARD IS BEING
OFFERED BY MR. TWAIN FOR
BAMBINO'S SAFE RETURN TO
21 FIFTH AVENUE.

The next morning Sam stood at his billiards table, rolling balls to the far end. But this time they didn't come back.

"It's all my fault, Jean," he said. "How will I explain this to Clara? Your sister will be so upset."

"Don't worry, Papa," Jean said, putting her arm around him. "I'm sure someone will see the announcements and return Bambino to us."

Soon a steady stream of people appeared on Sam's doorstep with cats and kittens of every size, color, and breed.

"Mr. Twain," a little girl said. "I read about your cat. Maybe you'd like to have ours until you get Bambino back?"

Sam was stunned. "But this is your family's beloved pet."

"We can spare him for a few days," she said, "if it keeps you from being sad."

"We also wanted to meet you," the girl's brother said.

"Thank you." Sam's voice cracked. "But . . . if Bambino does return, I don't think he'd take kindly to finding a foreign cat in his kingdom."

Even so, Sam's admirers continued to bring cats to their favorite author. Reporters from all over came to write about Mark Twain's missing Bambino. And this time Sam talked to them.

Three days passed with no sign of Bambino. Then, on the fourth morning, Katy went outside to get the newspaper. Sitting on the front walk was Bambino, grooming himself and unconcerned about the commotion he had caused.

"Wicked cat, to cause Mr. Clemens and Miss Jean so much worry!" Katy scolded as she grabbed Bambino by the scruff of the neck and carried him inside.

"The prodigal cat has returned! To celebrate, we'll feast on the fatted salmon!" Sam announced. Holding the cat close, he whispered, "Bambino, you've taught me a valuable lesson. There's a whole world outside of this house to enjoy."

Bambino blinked his blue eyes at Sam and touched a paw to his face.

An announcement about Bambino's return was placed in all the newspapers. But that didn't stop Sam's admirers. People dropped by to tell him how pleased they were about the cat's return. Sam greeted each visitor with a smile.

Sam kept his promise to Bambino and returned to the public world he loved. He had several white suits made and wore them year-round as his trademark. And he and Jean were reunited with Clara at their Stormfield home in Connecticut, where he hosted a musical gala.

". . . As to being on the verge of being a sick man, I don't take any stock in that. I have been on the verge of being an angel all my life, but it's never happened yet."

"Look at Papa," Clara whispered. "He's acting younger than I feel."

"He looks happier than he's been in a long time," Jean whispered back, putting an arm around her sister.

Bambino blinked his blue eyes and purred.

Author's Note

In November 1904 Samuel L. Clemens—known to the world by his pen name, Mark Twain—moved to 21 Fifth Avenue, New York City. Joining him was his youngest daughter, Jean; his housekeeper, Katy Leary; and a black cat named Bambino. Bambino was the pet of Clara Clemens, Sam's older daughter, who was in a clinic recovering from grief and stress caused by her mother's death. Because she could not have a cat with her in the clinic, she gave Bambino to her father.

Five months before *Bambino and Mr. Twain* starts, Sam's wife, Olivia ("Livy"), died. Not only were they deeply in love, but Livy was also Sam's editor. She helped Sam bring *Tom Sawyer, Huckleberry Finn,* and his other classic stories to life. When Livy died, Sam felt as if his reason for writing had died, too. When Sam moved to the Fifth Avenue house, he closed his door to the world.

But in the spring of 1905, everything changed when Bambino, who had been Sam's constant companion, disappeared out an open window. Just as in my story, an announcement was placed in all the newspapers, along with the offer of a five-dollar reward—which, back then, was a week's wages for most people. Many did see the announcement and brought their cats to be given or loaned to Sam as a way to show their affection.

Then, just as suddenly as he had disappeared, Bambino returned. But even after Sam placed the second announcement in the papers, people continued to bring cats to his home as a way to meet their favorite author.

A few months after Bambino's return, Sam took to wearing all-white suits year-round—a reminder of the suits he wore during the summers of his happier days when his entire family was alive. This is often how he is remembered today. Whether Bambino's return really had anything to do with Sam's decision is something only Sam and Bambino would know.

Bibliography

Clemens, Clara. *My Father, Mark Twain*. New York: Harper, 1931.

Lawton, Mary. *A Lifetime with Mark Twain: The Memories of Katy Leary, for Thirty Years His Faithful and Devoted Servant*. Whitefish, MT: Kessinger Publishing LLC, 2008. First published 1925 by Harcourt Brace.

Powers, Ron. *Mark Twain, A Life*. New York: Free Press, 2006.

Ward, Geoffrey C., Ken Burns, and Dayton Duncan. *Mark Twain: An Illustrated Biography*. New York: Knopf, 2001.